Walt Disney's
AMERICAN CLASSICS
Casey at the Bat

Based on the poem by Ernest Lawrence Thayer

Twin Books

MALLARD
PRESS

This is the story of a player who was the greatest of the great. He stood head and shoulders above all other players, a giant, a tower of strength and a true pillar of his team!

Strong as an ox, endowed with a winning smile and the abilities of ten lesser men, he was adored by many a fan. He was none other than The Mighty Casey of the famous Mudville Nine!

5

This mighty Casey popped the stitches on
more baseballs than most batters ever even hit!
Whenever he came to the plate, he would
always let the first two pitches go by—on purpose.
"*Strike one!*"
"*Strike two!*"

But when the time came for strike three, Casey would tire of toying with the pitcher. Grim determination would set in. He would grind his teeth together, and his furious glare said he wanted to murder the ball! Then came the pitch.

Casey swung his bat with the power of a hurricane!

9

When Casey's bat connected with the ball, hats blew off from the shock, and everyone ducked down low. Terrified birds flapped, and people's peanuts flew out of their bags!

If the ball didn't simply explode into a small cloud of horsehide flakes, it was found far outside the stadium—when it was found at all. It wasn't hard to prove which balls were from the mighty Casey's hits—they'd be completely flattened by his mighty bat!

Casey was great, but his team as a whole was a different story.

Poor Flynn was always getting the bat tangled in his oversized moustache. The bat would spin in the wind and the confused Flynn would take off like an airplane!

And as for Jimmy Blake, his nickname was "Cake" because he always crumbled on the plate.

A favorite trick among other players was to stick a match in
Jimmy Blake's shoe while he was at bat. Then they'd light it to wake
him up!
Blake got his only hits when his shoe was on fire.

Mighty Casey was the hero of the team that fateful season when the Mudville Nine tied for first place. Ah, yes, it was a proud team— a little shaky if it weren't for Casey, but a mighty proud team just the same! Proudest of all, of course, was Casey himself.

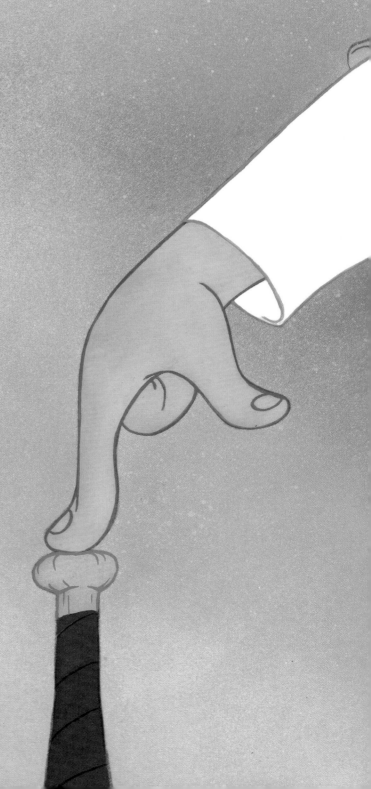

It was the day of the great Championship Game. I'll tell you the story as it was told to me:

The outlook wasn't brilliant for the Mudville Nine that day:
The score stood four to two with but one more inning left to play.
And then when Cooney died at first, and Barrows did the same,
A sickly silence fell upon the patrons of the game.

A straggling few got up to go in deep despair. The rest clung to that hope which springs eternal in the human breast. They thought, "If only Casey could but get a whack at that, we'd put up even money now, with Casey at the bat."

But Flynn preceded Casey, as did also Jimmy Blake,
And the former was a lulu and the latter was a cake;
So upon that stricken multitude grim melancholy sat,
For there seemed but little chance of Casey's getting to the bat.

But Flynn let drive a single,
    to the wonderment of all,
And Blake, the much despised,
    tore the cover off the ball;
And when the dust had lifted,
    and the men saw what had occurred,
There was Jimmy safe at second
    and Flynn a-hugging third.

Then from five thousand throats
    and more there rose a lusty yell;
It rumbled through the valley,
    it rattled in the dell;
It knocked upon the mountain
    and recoiled upon the flat...

… For Casey, mighty Casey,
   was advancing to the bat.

There was ease in Casey's manner
   as he stepped into his place;
There was pride in Casey's bearing
   and a smile on Casey's face.
And when, responding to the cheers,
   he lightly doffed his hat,
No stranger in the crowd could doubt
   'twas Casey at the bat.

Ten thousand eyes were on him as he rubbed his hands with dirt;
Five thousand tongues applauded when he wiped them on his shirt.
Then while the writhing pitcher ground the ball into his hip,
Defiance gleamed in Casey's eye, a sneer curled Casey's lip.

And now the leather-covered sphere came hurtling through the air,
  the air,
And Casey stood a-watching it in haughty grandeur there.
Close by the sturdy batsman the ball unheeded sped.

"That ain't my style," said Casey. "Strike one," the umpire
  said.

31

From the benches, black with people,
   there went up a muffled roar,
Like the beating of the storm-waves
   on a stern and distant shore.
"Kill him! Kill the umpire!"
   shouted someone in the stand;
And it's likely they'd have killed him
   had not Casey raised his hand.

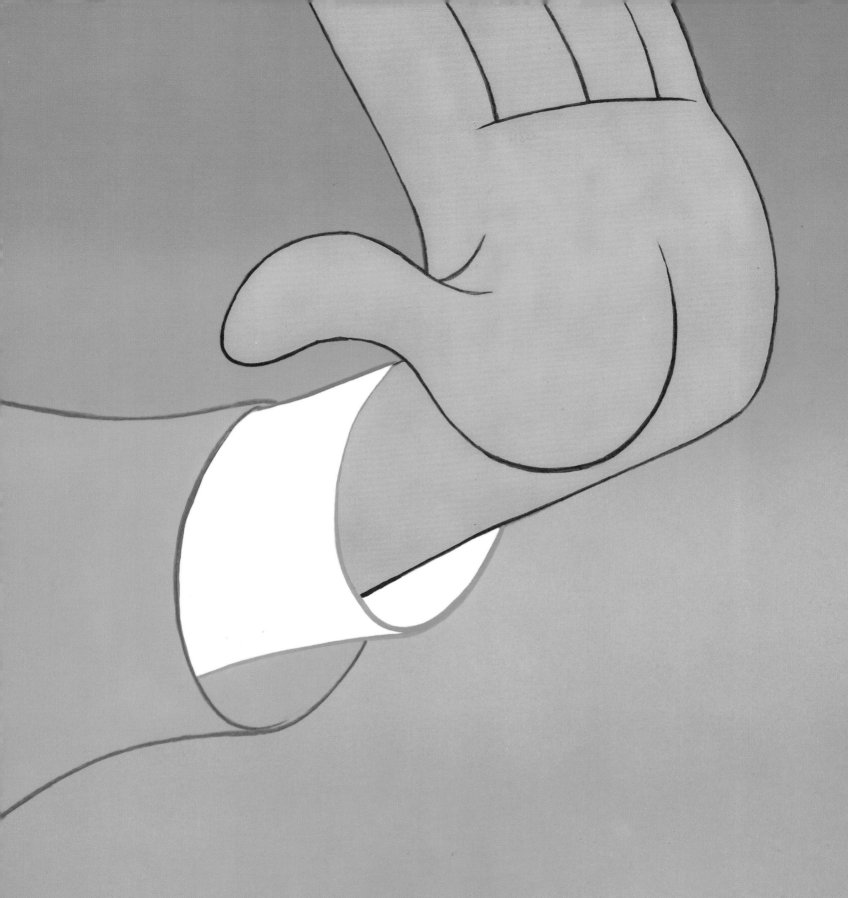

With a smile of Christian charity great Casey's visage shone;
He stilled the rising tumult; he bade the game go on;
He signalled to the pitcher, and once more the spheroid flew;
But Casey still ignored it, and the umpire said, "Strike two."
"Fraud!" cried the maddened thousands, and echo answered
  "Fraud";
But one scornful look from Casey and the audience was awed.

They saw his face grow stern and cold; they saw his muscles strain,
And they knew that Casey wouldn't let the ball go by again.
The sneer is gone from Casey's lip, his teeth are clenched in hate;
He pounds with cruel violence his bat upon the plate.

And now the pitcher holds the ball, and now he lets it go,
And the air is shattered by the force of Casey's blow.

Oh, somewhere in this favored land the sun is shining bright;
The band is playing somewhere, and somewhere hearts are light,
And somewhere men are laughing, and somewhere children shout;

But there is no joy in Mudville...
mighty Casey has struck out.

First published in the United States of
America in 1989 by The Mallard Press.

Mallard Press and its accompanying design
and logo are trademarks of
BDD Promotional Book Company, Inc.

Produced by
Twin Books
15 Sherwood Place
Greenwich, CT 06830

ISBN 0-792-45051-5

Designed, edited and illustrated by
American Graphic Systems, San Francisco

Printed in Hong Kong